Shutterbug Books
MATH
Steck-Vaughn

Looking for Patterns

by Ellen A. Goodenow

STECK-VAUGHN

Harcourt Supplemental Publishers

www.steck-vaughn.com

You can find patterns all around you.

All patterns have parts that repeat over and over.

Some patterns are made of different colors.
Where might you find this pattern?

This pattern is on a butterfly.
The different colors make a pattern on the wings.

Some patterns are made of shapes.
Where might you find this pattern?

This pattern is on a sunflower.
Tiny star shapes make this pattern.

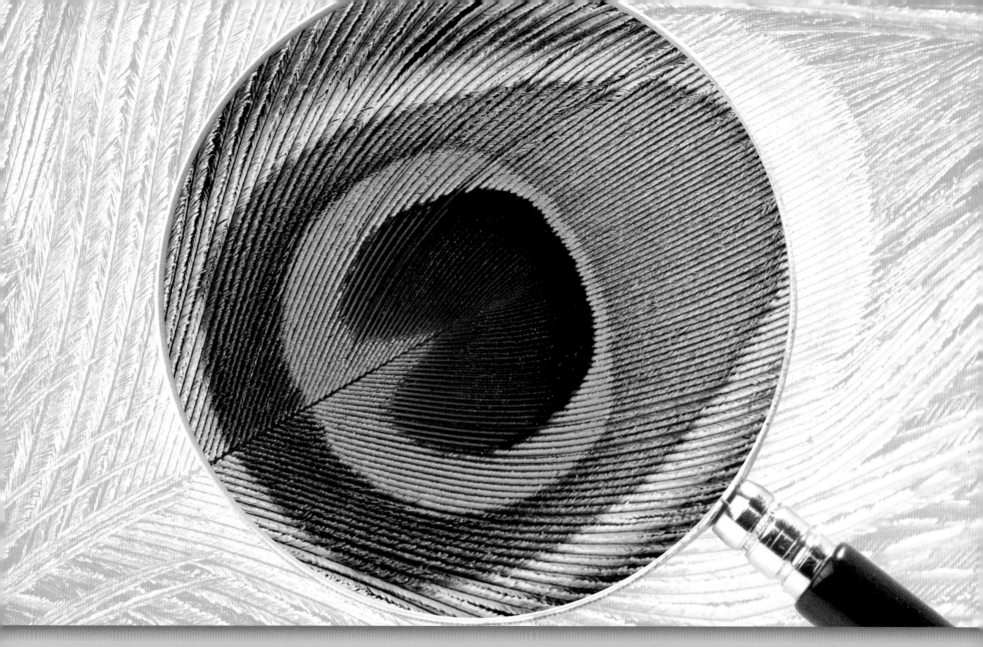

Some patterns are made of colors and shapes.
Where might you find this pattern?

This pattern is on a peacock's tail.
Colorful feathers make this pattern.

A spiral is another kind of pattern.
Where might you find this pattern?

This pattern is on a chameleon's tail.

Its tail is curled in a spiral pattern.

Size is important in some patterns.
Where might you find this pattern?

This pattern is on a shell.

The sections get bigger and bigger as the shell grows.

Some patterns are one of a kind.
Where might you find this pattern?

This pattern is on a snowflake.

Each snowflake is a little different from all other snowflakes.

Sometimes you can find different patterns in one place.
Where might you find these patterns?

These color and shape patterns are on the United States flag!
What other patterns can you see?